Bibliographical Series
of Supplements to 'British Book News'
on Writers and Their Work

★

GENERAL EDITOR
Bonamy Dobrée

CHARLES LAMB
from a portrait by R. Hancock *in pencil and chalk,
in the National Portrait Gallery*

CHARLES LAMB

by

EDMUND BLUNDEN

PUBLISHED FOR
THE BRITISH COUNCIL
AND THE NATIONAL BOOK LEAGUE
BY LONGMANS, GREEN & CO.

LONGMANS, GREEN & CO. LTD.
48 Grosvenor Street, London W.1

*Associated companies, branches and
representatives throughout the world*

First published 1960
Revised edition 1964
Revised edition, © Edmund Blunden, 1964

*Printed in Great Britain by
F. Mildner & Sons, London, E.C.1*

CONTENTS

CHARLES LAMB

I INTRODUCTION

IN NOVEMBER 1835 William Wordsworth, a man who can hardly be described as effusive, wrote a poem which was printed as his 'Extempore Effusion on the Death of the Ettrick Shepherd'—that is, the then well-known author James Hogg. The poem was of a wider scope than the title suggests, for Hogg was one of a series of poets over whom the grave had lately closed, leaving Wordsworth in old age and in a mood of isolation. His stanzas accordingly formed a lament for all these, whom he had known, and among them two had been friends from childhood until death. One was S. T. Coleridge; the other was mentioned thus, next to him:

> And Lamb, the frolic and the gentle,
> Has vanished from his lonely hearth.

It was also desired of Wordsworth as the master-poet and surviving friend that he should compose an epitaph for Lamb's gravestone. As he says, he missed that aim, but he hit another mark by completing a lengthy meditation on Lamb's history and personality, from which the following passage is taken:

> So genius triumphed over seeming wrong,
> And poured out truth in works by thoughtful love
> Inspired—works potent over smiles and tears.
> And as round mountain tops the lightning plays,
> Thus innocently sported, breaking forth
> As from a cloud of some grave sympathy,
> Humour and wild instinctive wit, and all
> The vivid flashes of his spoken words.

These tributes were not the first of Wordsworth's public expressions of his attitude towards Charles Lamb. Another, in courteous prose, had accompanied the narrative poem

7

called 'The Waggoner' in 1819; it was indeed the dedica-
tion of that long-withheld work, and Wordsworth gave
as his main reason for dedicating it to Lamb the 'acknow-
ledgement of the pleasure I have derived from your Writings and of the high esteem with which I am   Very truly
yours, William Wordsworth'.

It is easy to understand that, as time goes on, critical com-
mentary on Lamb is often based virtually upon the celebrated essays which he put forth over the signature 'Elia'.
Wordsworth probably had those papers chiefly in mind
when he wrote the passage on Lamb's genius defeating hard
circumstance which has been quoted. The 'Essays of Elia',
however, did not begin to appear in The *London Magazine*
before 1820, and we have seen that Wordsworth had already
done honour to Lamb as a writer. The compliment in 'The
Waggoner', 1819, was almost certainly called forth by
Lamb's *Works* in two volumes edited by some of his friends
the year before. These volumes did not sell in large numbers,
but they were prized by good judges of literature of whom
Wordsworth was one. The fact alone requires that Lamb's
literary life and experiments should be looked at by those
who desire to estimate him, to enjoy his pages, or to do
both on a plan extending beyond the limits of the two series
of *Essays of Elia*. The present sketch is intended as a help
towards such an ampler appreciation.

Lamb never made authorship his profession, and yet during forty years largely spent in accountancy and other
business of the East India Company he wrote and printed an
abundance of varied literary pieces. Sometimes, to increase
his chances of an occasional holiday excursion if for no
deeper reason, he played the journalist; and his friends who
edited newspapers or magazines were glad to have his
articles. He lost sight of many of those, but others remembered many long after their first purpose was served. He
wrote for the theatre. With his sister or alone he wrote
prose and verse for children; sometimes he ventured into
the field of critical disquisition, and examined the principles

of greatness in art as in literature. His serious poetry began when he was a schoolboy and was never afterwards far from his desire. Thus, without methodical intention, Lamb left writings enough to make him appear almost voluminous in the collected editions. While the *Essays of Elia* cannot be denied the central and highest part in his achievement, his readers can make many discoveries elsewhere in those volumes. Had the disguise or dramatization of Elia never occurred to him, Lamb would still have had his place in the annals of English authorship by virtue of different contributions: by his remarks on Shakespeare and the dramatists of Shakespeare's age whose excellences he especially revealed, his delineations of the stage and its performers in his own age, a number of inimitable poems in contrasting moods, and (to abridge the list) his often flowing imaginative and warm-hearted letters. It is sad that the very best of those which he wrote to the Wordsworths disappeared and evaded their search in early days.

II. EARLY INFLUENCES

In those instances where the heredity and the early life of an author are well recorded, it is not easy always to connect them with his literary turn or bent. We know something of John Lamb, Charles's father, and can at least note that he wrote and published verses in the middle of the eighteenth century; his three children, John, Mary, and Charles all had the trick of verse (and all wrote prose with feeling). The *Poetical Pieces* of John Lamb the elder were written, mostly in humorous style, for a small Friendly Society of which he was 'Laureate'. Beyond its members few people can have distinguished the clever rhymer in the man whose daily work was that of a clerk and steward. Mr. Lamb was officially a 'scrivener', worked in the Inner Temple which was and is one of the law colleges of London, and lived there in the house and the service of the generous Samuel Salt, Esq.

Mr. Lamb and his wife Elizabeth had seven children,

three of whom grew up. John the younger was born in 1763, Mary Anne in 1764, and the last of the seven, Charles, on 10 February 1775. At that date John was a scholar at Christ's Hospital, the ancient school for London children of needy parents that stood no great way from St. Paul's Cathedral; and John was therefore usually from home. When he came he was a self-centred and citified youth, and it was to Mary that the child Charles looked for companionship, given indeed with the greatest joy. The understanding endured as long as Lamb lived, and made its impression through the written word on his own and on later generations, at home and beyond seas. It endured inescapable trials which in the lifetime of Charles and Mary were kept as secret as possible, but which, now that they are noticed in every biography, may suggest that the artist does not always devote himself to pleasing the world but sometimes to defying the outer darkness.

To pass through the Temple even now, if the weather is sweet, is to experience something of that retirement from the mill of life which Lamb, as Elia, beautifully illustrated. 'Its church, its halls, its gardens, its fountain, its river!' Even in that essay on 'The Old Benchers of the Inner Temple' he had to complain of alterations, of fountains choked, sundials removed, and (almost worse) dignities and sacrednesses overwhelmed. His essay explains in its measure the kind of garden beauty which was his solace and something more through life, and the singular observancy of the beloved setting and moment which he maintained in other places. Then, 'my first hint of allegory' was here. Nobody excels Lamb in the power of perceiving the symbol or the outward sign of the inward or the visionary grace. But the title 'The Old Benchers of the Inner Temple' appears to imply that in his childhood there he became prepared for another interest of his maturity, the enjoyment and the portrayal of human character. If we conjecture that when he came to describing those wonderful magnificos who formerly paraded the Terrace in the Temple he partly worked in the reminiscences of his sister, we do not fall into any gross improbability.

Among the Benchers Lamb presents 'the pensive gentility of Samuel Salt', and well he might; for he was born in Samuel Salt's house, and that house was as much the child's as the Temple itself. The good barrister, as Lamb's best follower E. V. Lucas pointed out, 'gave to Charles and Mary the freedom of his library, . . . a privilege which, to ourselves, is the most important of all'. Lamb, in general, had a theory that children should not be shepherded into reading only pretty little books designed for their presumed limitations or appetites, but let loose among 'good old English reading, without much selection or prohibition'; and Mr. Salt the barrister seems to have come to the same conclusion in his day. It was, however, not in Salt's shelves but in Lamb's father's 'book-closet' that the small boy encountered an immense work, bound up after being bought in instalments, called Stackhouse's *History of the Bible*. This monster consists in part of illustrations, and one of them, showing the Witch of Endor raising up the phantasm of Samuel, tormented Charles Lamb's nightly fancy from his fourth year to his seventh. At last he poked his finger by mishap through the ridiculous picture of Noah's Ark in the said Stackhouse, and was forbidden to unclose that book again.

In his seventh year Lamb was being considered for a privilege both valuable and formidable. He was to exchange his first simple school for that which had equipped his elder brother for a safe job in the South Sea House. Mr. Salt was one of those good-natured men who have had a passion for enriching Christ's Hospital and, as governors, securing education in that House for promising but necessitous boys and girls. The House had been founded by King Edward VI (and the City of London) in the Reformation; a monastery had been converted into a school; and the school had become a source of strength for the Church, the Universities, the teaching world, and above all the commercial City.

Lamb might even become a sea captain, in the Royal Navy or in trade, if he was admitted. He was admitted, and 'clothed'—in the blue coat and yellow stockings still worn by Christ's Hospital boys—on 9 October 1782. His attainments were such that he was at once included in the senior school, a mile or less from home; and at the same time one Samuel Taylor Coleridge from distant Devonshire was sent there.

Some of the distresses which children like Coleridge might feel in the strange and gigantic school, before they found their way in it, were narrated by Lamb in one of his *Elia* essays, but this was mainly an instance of his imaginative sympathy. He had long before summed up his own schooldays as 'joyful'. If the daily routine of Christ's Hospital had been bitter to him, as it seems it was to others, he could count on being in the Temple and among his consolations at least twice a week. But he found Christ's Hospital as romantic as the Temple though less spacious and flowergrown. Its cloisters alone were a noble antiquity. The hall was noble, and its walls were hung with great pictures of royal and other benefactors, still seeming to watch over the destinies of their Bluecoat boys. If the diet prescribed was not such as boys could call good, yet Lamb was not much concerned, for his aunt Hetty would soon be plodding into the quadrangles with her basket of interesting food from the Temple. It is not known that this boy ever met with the sharp violence which others aroused by misdeeds or misfortune; he observed the tyranny of the upper grammar master, Dr. Boyer, and the toughness of the mathematical head, William Wales, F.R.S., almost as an envoy from another country. Here too, we may say, Lamb fed on character.

Coleridge was speedily selected by Dr. Boyer as a boy to be trained for the University, and at that period Christ's Hospital could only foster a few of them at a time. However often Coleridge was thundered at and flogged, he remained to be head of the school, and to be sent to Cambridge with an extraordinary reputation already. Boyer did not overlook Lamb, who was three years younger, and yet perceived the genius of his friend Coleridge. Lamb was not of the same versatility, but he was a capital classic as far as his years allowed, and his English compositions were precise and sensible. It was a mystery to later generations of studious Blues that Lamb had not been made a Grecian, or sixth-form boy, and many declared that he had been one; but at the point when he might have been promoted, and so set on the road to a University career, some impediment appeared. An impediment in his speech, some say; others believe that the comparative poverty of his parents obliged him to turn away from 'the sweet food of academic institution' and follow his brother John out of Christ's Hospital into city life. Nothing was easier then for a Blue of good report. Yet all through his city life something of the collegian persisted in Lamb's outlook and spoke in his writings, even if in a humorist's accents; if he had a perpetual sadness, this disappointment after his exemplary studies at Christ's Hospital was part of it.

Lamb was at the school from 1782 to 1789. It was at one of its highest points, if the energetic lives and achievements of many of its alumni are acceptable as evidence. They did well in all sorts of professions and enterprises, and nowhere more than in literature, classical and original. Most of those writers are forgotten now in the mass of ingenious productions which their period called for, but in some one may catch certain likenesses to Lamb. And this may be connected with what he himself interpreted, the character of the boys in their cloistered school, their Tudor costume, their dependence and independence, their responsibility to a generous nursing-mother, their ceremonies and courtesies, their unity in variety, their dream of returning to their old House as good men who would spur on the latest comers in it. Lamb tells us that the Christ's Hospital boy's friends were commonly his friends through life, and Coleridge was not his only reason for saying so, nor was he thinking of his own circle only.

The contrast between the two chief classical masters who both taught in the old Grammar School at Christ's Hospital amused Lamb and his contemporaries, and thanks to him will amuse readers still to come; he is laughing at Coleridge as he writes, for Coleridge was at the unlucky end of the stick.

The Upper and Lower Grammar Schools were held in the same room; and an imaginary line only divided their bounds. Their character was as different as that of the inhabitants on the two sides of the Pyrenees. The Rev. James Boyer was the Upper Master: but the Rev. Matthew Field presided over that portion of the apartment, of which I had the good fortune to be a member. We lived a life as careless as birds. We talked and did just what we pleased, and nobody molested us. We carried an accidence, or a grammar, for form; but, for any trouble it gave us, we might take two years in getting through the verbs deponent, and another two in forgetting all that we had learned about them. There was now and then the formality of saying a lesson, but if you had not learned it, a brush across the shoulders (just enough to disturb a fly) was the sole remonstrance. Field never used the rod; and in truth he wielded the cane with no great good will—holding it 'like a dancer'. It looked in his hands rather like an emblem than an instrument of authority; and an emblem, too, he was ashamed of. He was a good easy man, that did not care to ruffle his own peace, nor perhaps set any great consideration upon the value of juvenile time. He came among us, now and then, but often stayed away whole days from us; and when he came, it made no difference to us—he had his private room to retire to, the short time he stayed, to be out of the sound of our noise.

But then:

Though sufficiently removed from the jurisdiction of Boyer, we were near enough (as I have said) to understand a little of his system. We occasionally heard sounds of the *Ululantes*, and caught glances of Tartarus. B. was a rabid pedant. His English style was cramped to barbarism. His Easter anthems (for his duty obliged him to those periodical flights) were grating as scrannel pipes—He would laugh, ay, and heartily, but then it must be at Flaccus's quibble about *Rex*—or at the *tristis severitas in vultu*, or *inspicere in patinas*, of Terence—thin jests, which at their first broaching could hardly have had *vis* enough to move a Roman muscle.—He had two wigs, both pedantic, but of different omen. The one serene, smiling, fresh powdered, betokening a mild day. The other, an old discoloured unkempt angry caxon, denoting frequent and bloody execution. Woe to the school, when he made his morning appearance in his *passy*, or *passionate wig*. No comet expounded surer.

'Christ's Hospital Five and Thirty Years Ago' (*Essays of Elia*).

So far we have only looked at the child Lamb in London, and some would have it (he was apt to take this line himself) that he was absolutely a Londoner. But his mother is the refutation of this. Elizabeth Field was a village girl. In Hertfordshire even now there may be rural relatives of Lamb, and country corners where he once paused as not quite a townee. His grandmother, Mrs. Field, who was housekeeper at Blakesware House, a residence of almost too great a charm to think of now, did not forget the Lamb children. Hence, before and during his Christ's Hospital days, Charles was transferred northward by coach away from London's din and even the Temple's pomps into the summer's own country, into the sleepy great house and all its museum of relics and treasures of art, and whatever its lawns, copses, ponds, and running waters comprehended. If he could, Lamb would take with him a schoolfellow whose means were insufficient for his longer journey home. At 'Blakesmoor', an estate since unmade, Lamb was a country child, and so he was elsewhere on occasion; nevertheless, it was a place that very curiously continued the chain of his first experiences. 'From cloister to cloister' he passed from the Inner Temple to Christ's Hospital; and when he sought out the essence of his holidays in the country mansion which his grandmother had as if it were hers, things were much the same. His reflections after many years are undeniably Lamb's own even if they were offered as Elia's:

The solitude of childhood is not so much the mother of thought, as it is the feeder of love, and silence, and admiration. So strange a passion for the place possessed me in those years, that, though there lay—I shame to say how few roods distant from the mansion—half hid by trees, what I judged some romantic lake, such was the spell which bound me to the house, and such my carefulness not to pass its strict and proper precincts, that the idle waters lay unexplored for me. . . . So far from a wish to roam, I would have drawn, methought, still closer the fences of my chosen prison; and have been hemmed in by a yet securer cincture of those excluding garden walls.

  'Blakesmoor in H———shire' (*Last Essays of Elia*.)

Lamb did not need to go very far in order to betray himself in another aspect to anybody with eyes to see. Not so long after the death of the lady, Mrs. Plumer, to whom his 'Blakesmoor' belonged, he must have written one of his first letters to his grandmother, inviting, on her behalf, himself and friend to stay with her. The friend was a Blue-coat boy of no little ability, at school the rival of Coleridge, and afterwards a man of wealth who delighted in his famous friends. Charles Valentine Le Grice (to name him) remembered how Lamb had persuaded him to 'Blakesmoor', and when the two were there, how his junior had shown him round until they came to the stables. There on the wall was hanging the harness that had been used for Mrs. Plumer's carriage. Le Grice (then growing old) recorded how Charles Lamb had drawn his attention to it and to the fact that it was never to be used again, and added how much he had felt the seriousness of this communication from so young a boy.

III. A YOUNG POET

When Lamb was about to leave Christ's Hospital, the headmaster gave him the chief distinction—as Lamb and his schoolfellows would think—that he could. There was an almost sacred book in Dr. Boyer's keeping, into which he would sometimes request his top boys to transcribe their English essays or poems, and very occasionally one of the class below. It was a poem that Lamb was desired to add to this remarkable anthology. The metre is good, the style correct, on eighteenth-century lines; but it is a piece in which an odd humour plays across a 'vision' of mortality. Thus in 1789 Lamb showed the wit-melancholy which became subtle in years burdened with experience. We have unfortunately no portrait of the boy Lamb.

To what degree is it sound to build on the fact that Lamb's first known writing is a poem? At least we see him for the next ten years or so continuing, with a natural hesitancy, to live inwardly and to try his genius in expression as a young poet. The period itself, from 1789 to 1798, if such dates assist us, was a curious time for English poetry; while it was difficult to name any mighty contemporary masters, there was a widespread newness of sensitive and psychological verse by men and women too. In its profound development, as time unfolded, this preoccupation became obvious and conspicuous as the Romantic Movement in England, and one small volume by Coleridge and Wordsworth in 1798 was to take rank as the special ordinance of it all. One or two forms of verse, which had been gaining ground in Dr. Johnson's days—he must have seen Charles Lamb as a child among the children in the Temple—and which he had deplored as a mere mode, were beloved by the young poets of sensibility in that period. They were: blank verse, and the sonnet, the meditation in fourteen lines of rhyme. Lamb was content with both.

Here we may interpose a few details of his career. Not being allowed to follow Coleridge to Cambridge, Lamb was first shown counting-house duties in the office of Joseph Paice, a merchant of unsurpassed gentleness; thence he was sent to the South Sea House, where his forceful brother John was prospering; and next to the East India House, through the influence it is believed of Samuel Salt. In the India House, as the world knows, Charles Lamb remained, and his portrait remains. His clerkship there began in 1792, and the presumptions that he idled and anticked through that official world is wrong. From the first he had to consider, and he did consider, a great deal of work and a great complexity of personalities and conventions. Lamb in his published allusions to his office work surrounds it with a profusion of fancy and jest, but in reality he so studied it as to become a sort of hero to his successors—their superior, and their companion.

Samuel Salt died in 1792, and the Lamb family mainly living on bequests had to leave their home in the Temple. It was a household such as perhaps some French novelist might best have represented. It was most hospitable, most intelligent; but poor John Lamb the Elder was losing his mind. His sister, 'Aunt Hetty', was loving, simple, unnecessary. His wife, Elizabeth, was socially remote from her, but her strong character came out most in rebuffs for Mary her own daughter. Charles had his own calls on Mary's uncommon unselfishness; he confided in her while he was in love with a 'fair-hair'd maid' in the Hertfordshire they knew so well together, and when that dream was fading. But, it may be judged, Mary herself had a love, and had nobody to tell it to—and then, she was overworked as a 'mantua-maker' and even as a teacher of dress-making. All this and much else came to a head 'in a day of horrors' in September 1796. That day, Charles Lamb on his way to the office had tried to catch the family physician, so that he might call on Mary, who had been suspiciously quiet. When he returned home, he found Mary brandishing a carving knife over the mother whom she had just stabbed to death, after failing to slay her screaming apprentice.

The madness of which this was the tragic discovery never passed away, but was not incessant. Charles, who did what his elder brother probably ought to have done, accepted the guardianship of his sister, and that was in the end a security for all that was great in himself. Their father died in 1799 and thenceforward it was Charles and Mary Lamb.

At this point we resume the theme of Lamb as a young poet—a character which in the winter of 1796 he declared he had cast away from him for ever with other vanities, but soon found to be a necessity. Probably he destroyed some notebooks, and we have no great quantity of his early work. He published some of it in Coleridge's *Poems on Various Subjects*, 1796 and 1797, some more in Charles Lloyd's *Poems on the Death of Priscilla Farmer* in 1796 and in *Blank Verse*, 1798, where his name appeared with Lloyd's on the title-page, and for some time he contributed to a new and agreeable periodical, *The Monthly Magazine*. These appearances and his association with two young poets of a slightly revolutionary outlook in politics called some attention to his name. The delicacy and the religious quality of his poetry made their appeal to a few readers. Coleridge both encouraged and disheartened him, being still his senior in the fashion of their schooldays and by his restless power and ideas now praising, now rewriting, at last burlesquing Lamb's verses. It was not so much the literary criticism implied that distressed Lamb as the obscuring of his own honestly uttered feelings.

These sonnets of lost or fancied love, these soliloquies on altered fortune, on family history, on friendship and on loneliness, on the mystery of things and the eternal foundations of man in the divine, form altogether quite an individual 'progress' of poetry. Lamb had not then the art of original bold observation or peculiar novelty of phrase, but was happy in a general and melodious simplicity; and sometimes his simple lines excelled in their places for the emotion they conveyed,

> I passed the little cottage which she loved . . .
> Beloved, who shall tell me where thou art? . . .
> How shall we tell them in a stranger's ear? . . .

Such unforced speech, in its right order, may go deep. In January 1798 Lamb seemed to sum up what he had known of life, with its vicissitudes, in the impromptu which became a classic, 'The Old Familiar Faces'. He had amused himself with light verses in the Latin metre then being adapted to English poetry by his friend Southey and others, and

suddenly when a new disappointment in friendship was on
his mind the thought of the past fitted the tune exactly:

> All, all are gone, the old familiar faces.

It was not literally true, but it was for him the adieu to
youth. It was composed in the Temple.

One of the characteristics of Lamb's literary company
was that most were devoted to English authors of a remoter
time than their own century, then closing; from J. M.
Gutch with whom he sometime lodged, a Blue and an
editor, to William Godwin the political philosopher and
novelist, all of them had their idolatries of the ages of
Shakespeare and Milton. Lamb had many, and among these
'antiques' of his the dramatic poets of the early seventeenth
century stood out. It was a consequence easily to be under-
stood that in 1798 this young enthusiast began work on a
play in an old manner, entitled *Pride's Cure*, but subsequently
and on publication *John Woodvil*. It hardly asks to be judged
as drama now, but as a work of art—a form in which the
poet conveyed the sense of the qualities he loved in the old
plays, and something of himself besides. It was the brook-
clear style, not the robustious profusion that he still liked
most, and followed delightfully; here is one of Margaret's
speeches, or was it Lamb's Anna in Hertfordshire whom he
imagined speaking to himself?

> Dost yet remember the green arbour, John,
> In the south gardens of my father's house,
> Where we have seen the summer sun go down.
> Exchanging true love's vows without restraint?
> And that old wood, you call'd your wilderness,
> And vow'd in sport to build a chapel in it,
> There dwell
>   'Like hermit poor
>   In pensive place obscure',
> And tell your Ave Maries by the curls
> (Dropping like golden beads) of Margaret's hair;

And make confession seven times a day
Of every thought that stray'd from love and Margaret;
And I your saint the penance should appoint—
Believe me, sir, I will not now be laid
Aside, like an old fashion.

When *John Woodvil* was published, in 1802, the reviewers missed the point and ridiculed it, but they had their own ideas of Elizabethan tragedy, and Lamb called it 'a tragedy'. It was rather a study in a style, which demanded an aesthetic fineness more likely to be found in musical criticism than in the book-reveving organizations of Lamb's day. A host of neo-Elizabethan dramas was now being composed, and many were suited for the stage, but Lamb's 'variation' was not parallelled.

IV. PROSE ALSO

As in verse, so in prose: Lamb's first surviving attempts were marked by his responsiveness to style, and he had— from the old hours in Samuel Salt's library and through his book-hunting vacations—a discoverer's instinct that way. His own work might spring from this, usually not as imitation but as variation. We cannot say with certainty what Lamb's share was in a book published in 1796, *Original Letters &c. of Sir John Falstaff*, which in any case was principally the work of his schoolfellow and friend until death, James White. It was topical (a hit at the Shakespeare forgeries then flourishing) and it lives still. But Lamb openly presented as an appendix to *John Woodvil* his *Curious Fragments* as they might have been found in the old writer, Robert Burton, whose *Anatomy of Melancholy* always captures some tastes at any period.

Of greater importance and personal significance was *A Tale of Rosamund Gray and Old Blind Margaret*, written in 1797 and 1798, and published in the latter year. It is a kind of novel, though it would not occupy many more pages than this essay; and it was, however anxiously conceived as a story of innocence and calamity in the light of sensibility, an experiment in method and style. Something of Sterne's way of breaking off and beginning as if in another direction is in it, and more of Henry Mackenzie's 'fragmentary' narrative in brief; for Lamb had been reading, as so many had, *The Man of Feeling* and other things by Mackenzie. Lamb included much in this tale beyond the evident needs of telling it, and contrived to digress even in those narrow limits chosen for the whole; much in it was concise and homely, the humour was everyday, and yet there are interludes of romance and of speculation. It is seen that already his notion of prose was that it can be elaborate in design where the theme suggests a specially imaginative movement. The third chapter is a sort of song for Rosamund Gray, and then an invocation to the moon shining upon the writer's window which is harmonized with that song. But Lamb ends his book with a paragraph of four words only, 'Matravis died that night'.

Lamb picked up the name of the villain Matravis from one of his Elizabethan authors. To these, to the dramatists at least, he gave up much of his leisure from the India House, and after an immense range of intense reading he put forth in 1808 the most striking anthology perhaps ever made from English literature. It was called *Specimens of English Dramatic Poets*, and in later life Lamb read on and chose supplementary passages—for he could not pretend that his book was other than a masterpiece of inquiry into a magnificent and neglected subject. But it is noticed here with particular allusion to the prose notes which accompany the poetic selections. Whether they are invariably to be endorsed as canons of criticism is not my interest; indeed not much criticism is as likely to be accepted by all as the tide tables; the prose itself, sounding like the voice of a full intellectual and spiritual devotion, is noteworthy. 'Their dignity', Mr Frank Morley writes of those notes on Marlowe, Webster,

Chapman, and the rest, 'cannot be disregarded. They could not have been written except by a man of grave and energetic spirit; a spirit of larger motions than some have credited to Lamb.'

One of the most congenial criticisms thus delivered by Lamb was prompted by Thomas Middleton's play *The Witch* and some prevailing talk about Shakespear's indebtedness to Middleton. Lamb clears that away.

The Witch.—Though some resemblance may be traced between the charms in Macbeth, and the incantations in this play, which is supposed to have preceded it, this coincidence will not detract much from the originality of Shakespeare. His witches are distinguished from the witches of Middleton by essential differences. These are creatures to whom man or woman, plotting some dire mischief, might resort for occasional consultation. Those originate deeds of blood, and begin bad impulses to men. From the moment that their eyes first meet with Macbeth's, he is spell-bound. That meeting sways his destiny. He can never break the fascination. These witches can hurt the body, those have power over the soul. Hecate in Middleton has a son, a low buffoon: the hags of Shakespeare have neither child of their own, nor seem to be descended from any parent. They are foul anomalies, of whom we know not whence they are sprung, nor whether they have beginning or ending. As they are without human passions, so they seem to be without human relations. They come with thunder and lightning, and vanish to airy music. This is all we know of them. Except Hecate, they have no *names*; which heightens their mysteriousness. The names, and some of the properties, which the other author has given to his hags, excite smiles. The Weird Sisters are serious things. Their presence cannot co-exist with mirth. But, in a lesser degree, the witches of Middleton are fine creations. Their power too is, in some measure, over the mind. They raise jars, jealousies, strifes, 'like a thick scurf' over life.

'Characters of Dramatic Writers Contemporary with Shakespeare'
(*Miscellaneous Prose*).

It is the same with two long critical essays contributed by Lamb to a quarterly edited by Leigh Hunt in 1810–11, The *Reflector*: namely, 'On the Genius and Character of

Hogarth' and 'On the Tragedies of Shakespeare, Considered with reference to their Fitness for Stage Representation'. Both pieces were paradoxical, or aggressively unorthodox. Lamb set out to demonstrate that the common view of Hogarth 'as a mere comic painter, as one whose chief ambition was to *raise a laugh*', was wrong, and that instead Hogarth's works were a grand school of life. In the other paper he maintained that Shakespeare was reduced by the details of the material stage from that infinite scale on which he addresses the imagination of his reader. In both instances, whether we concede his argument or not, the vitality of the critic's mind and the abundance of his armoury brought into action with rapid freshness, and be it added the noble construction of the whole, are something beyond the ordinary. The two essays served at once as classics often quoted by Lamb's contemporaries.

Lamb expresses the difference between seeing Shakespeare acted and reading him in terms which must move us strongly, even if we do not accept the conclusion:

The state of sublime emotion into which we are elevated by those images of night and horror which Macbeth is made to utter, that solemn prelude with which he entertains the time till the bell shall strike which is to call him to murder Duncan,—when we no longer read it in a book, when we have given up that vantage-ground of abstraction which reading possesses over seeing, and come to see a man in his bodily shape before our eyes actually preparing to commit a murder, if the acting be true and impressive, as I have witnessed it in Mr. K.'s performance of that part, the painful anxiety about the act, the natural longing to prevent it while it yet seems unperpetrated, the too close pressing semblance of reality, give a pain and an uneasiness which totally destroy all the delight which the words in the book convey, where the deed doing never presses upon us with the painful sense of presence: it rather seems to belong to history—to something past and inevitable, if it has anything to do with time at all. The sublime images, the poetry alone, is that which is present to our minds in the reading.

> 'On the Tragedies of Shakespeare, Considered with Reference to their Fitness for Stage Representation' (*Miscellaneous Prose*).

Tales from Shakespeare, Mrs. Leicester's School, and the like, written before 1811, have carried the name of Charles and Mary Lamb into reading circles where his theories about Hogarth and Shakespeare do not arise. The *Tales*, undertaken for some desirable guineas, were completed with many groans, for Lamb saw that the task was really impossible; but as his sister commented, 'he has made something of it', and of her share people say the same.

V. *WORKS*, 1818

The first decade of the nineteenth century was passed by the Lambs mainly in their old home, the Temple, though for a time Lamb tried going off to a room or two away from it so that he might write with less interruption. His sister was sometimes absent for the more melancholy reason that her mind was occasionally darkened again; she herself well knew when she must place herself under restraint for a period. Her case is a strange one, indeed, since ordinarily she was recognized by their increasing circle of friends, famous or unmarked, as a woman of conspicuous wisdom and poise. She superintended while she enjoyed the great hospitality of the household; she was the counsellor of Coleridge, of Hazlitt, and among them all and foremost her brother himself. When she wrote, as in *Mrs. Leicester's School*, the calm beauty of her nature achieved completeness of style and story. Her few poems too were simple and wise.

The Lambs were theatre-goers and made friends with many men and women connected with the stage; it is not surprising that Lamb tried to write for it. A success there would have golden effects on the spirit of their days and on the question of paying their bills, for although Lamb was gradually rising in the ranks of the East India House clerks, the money came slowly in. In 1806 his farce *Mr. H——* was accepted at Drury Lane, and on 10 December it was acted. It contains plenty of amusing dialogue and light

satire, but depends on the delayed revelation of Mr. H——'s
name in full, and when it comes it is insufficient to justify all
the expectation. Consequently, the audience at Drury Lane
first applauded briskly, but when H—— was found to be
only Hogflesh they hissed, and so did the author, seated near
the orchestra. *Mr. H——* was withdrawn. Its failure was
very near indeed to a lasting popularity.

From Mitre Court Buildings the Lambs moved house,
but still within their accustomed range—to 4 Inner Temple
Lane, and remained until 1817. The plan of their life and its
work and play was unaltered. It allowed a number of
journeys and visitings outside London. Lamb's only sojourn
among Wordsworth's lakes and mountains had satisfied
Wordsworth that he could take delight in such scenes in
spite of his usual protestations, but probably his contentment
was fullest in less romantic regions, in the Thames valley for
example, or near the southern shores of England. Lamb
meanwhile produced his articles for newspapers and
miscellanies, and was valued by most who knew him not
only for those but for his conversation on writers and books.
Much of it, though not in all its original brilliance, is
sketched in the vast diary of his watchful friend Crabb
Robinson, who tried to make him read Goethe.

The sign of his being recognized as a 'great contemporary'
was the publication, arranged by others, of the two volumes
entitled his *Works* in 1818. Here were some poems to prove
that he had enlarged his scope and released his imagination
since 1798. The new sonnets were of a new energy. But the
longest of the poems was the best, and it won many ad-
mirers; it was 'A Farewell to Tobacco'. In metre it was a
revival of seventeenth-century verse, and like that too in
the play of the mind, moving swiftly from the homely and
colloquial to the far allusion and powerful fancy. The 'Great
Plant' there, as he said, made a bold attempt to overcome
the imagery of the god of the vine and grape.

One of the prose pieces was a typical appreciation of a
forgotten writer who, thanks largely to Lamb, has been

since a favourite. It was George Wither, the seventeenth-century poet, whom Lamb's schoolfellow Gutch collected and privately reprinted about 1810. The reader of this beautiful criticism will notice that Lamb was not merely a hunter of rare poetry in distant places, for he makes a comparison between the spirit of liberty in Wither and that in 'every page of our late glorious Burns'. Before long he was to read Keats and announce his excellences in a quite poetical review.

The biography of Lamb cannot be condensed here, but the reappearance of his sonnet to the actress Fanny Kelly in his *Works* requires the mention of one of its principal episodes. In 1819, having been secretly haunted by Miss Kelly's kind nature and unassuming genius for years, Lamb sent her his proposal of marriage: 'In many a sweet assumed character I have learned to love you, but simply as F. M. Kelly I love you better than them all. Can you quit these shadows of existence, and come and be a reality to us?' Much moved—for she was Lamb's friend—but seeing that such a marriage would involve her in the 'sad mental uncertainty which surrounded his domestic life', Miss Kelly declined him. Out of this disappointment, like others, Lamb appears even to have gained in fortitude, but perhaps towards his death the accumulation of 'failures' told on him.

VI. *ELIA* DEVELOPED

At the age of forty-five Lamb did not give his friends any impression that he was growing old, but he might well think with Emerson, 'It is time to be old', and further,

> A little while
> Still plan and smile,
> And, fault of novel germs,
> Mature the unfallen fruit.

For his personal life, it promised to go on with little change of design to the end, governed by the deep mutual dependence of Mary and himself, and in the next place by his genuine allegiance to the office at the India House which to him was as a company of soldiers to a good company commander. In literature, what more? One thing was certain; he could now look back on thirty, even on thirty-five years of love of human life, its changing scenes, its enigmatic presences, its men and women. From childhood he had been in his curious way a collector of characters, even of places.

When he was invited to contribute to The *London Magazine* of 1820, edited by John Scott, Lamb was certainly pleased; it was no casual offer. He was to have a regular place. Reminiscence would furnish him with materials enough for most of the monthly papers desired. The first of these appeared in August 1820, 'Recollections of the South-Sea House'—and Lamb, who does not oblige us with many peeps behind the screen concerning his literary methods, explains its signature 'Elia': 'a person of that name, an Italian, was a fellow clerk of mine at the South Sea House.' He says that he just used the name as a protection, in case his brother John still in that House were offended by 'certain descriptions' in the text. Yet Elia was, or became, more than a pseudonym. Elia too was a personality, for the purpose of these writings. The argument whether or not he was equivalent to Lamb's conception of himself will long continue.

So far as Elia is indicated as 'a phantom', a recluse living in the past and speaking in a language antique and remote, he may be described as an invention. He is to that extent a kinsman of such figures as the Spectator or the Gentleman in Black who had been devised by eighteenth-century essayists, and of the 'I' who is put forward to tell the tale of many a novel. But Lamb could not be so formal in his compositions as Addison and Steele, or his predecessor in the Temple, Goldsmith, and he neither imposed distinctness upon his 'poor gentleman' nor employed him or remembered his function with regularity in the essays signed Elia. In January 1823 Lamb tried to convince his friends and readers at large, by a farewell essay declaring that Elia was dead and gone, that he had carried on his fantasy as far as he wished or ought. It was not accepted; the name had become an attraction, and the humour and sadness which Elia's style had presented were regarded as Lamb's undoubted self-expression. He agreed that he had on occasion communicated his own story through the disguise, and noted that sometimes he had done the opposite.

The *London Magazine* passed from John Scott's hands to John Taylor's, and drifted thence again, so that Lamb's share in it ran from 1820 to 1825, but some papers from other and especially later magazines are gathered into *The Essays of Elia* as the book stands. It comprises two books arranged by Lamb himself, *Elia* (1823) and *The Last Essays of Elia* (1833), and the standard reached at once in the paper on the South Sea House was kept up surprisingly well to the last. It is true that *The Last Essays* ends with a set of comments on 'Popular Fallacies' which do not all attempt to be more than table-talk, but among them also Lamb shows his varied power, now describing the uniqueness of an outwardly ugly countenance, now movingly insisting that poverty is no blessing to childhood, presently arguing against early rising in a mood of approaching death. Apart from this series, *Elia* closes with no less an essay than 'Old China', wherein he uses to the fullest advantage his method of seeming but only seeming to desert his stated subject.

Lamb did not think that his critics were all wrong in objecting to the 'affected array of antique modes and phrases' of *Elia*; he hints that the trouble was not one of the choice of style but want of control of it. To dwell on Elianism for a moment, I reflect that it is sometimes elaborate and fanciful to a fault, but that it can be perfect in point and sound. Here are two paragraphs on two kinds of borrowers:

When I think of this man; his fiery glow of heart; his swell of feeling; how magnificent, how *ideal* he was; how great at the midnight hour;

and when I compare with him the companions with whom I have associated since, I grudge the saving of a few idle ducats, and think that I am fallen into the society of *lenders*, and *little men*.

To one like Elia, whose treasures are rather cased in leather covers than closed in iron coffers, there is a class of alienators more formidable than that which I have touched upon; I mean your *borrowers of books*—those mutilators of collections, spoilers of the symmetry of shelves, and creators of odd volumes. There is Comberbatch, matchless in his depredations!

'The Two Races of Men (*Essays of Elia*).

How could this mock-serious charge against the mighty Coleridge (who denied it) have been delivered better?

The manner and tune of the Essays is as changeful as their occasion and topic, for Lamb saw English prose as an instrument with stops enough for every use and grace. If he is moved to speak direct thoughts, he lets Elia go and is as laconic as can be. 'When I am not walking, I am reading; I cannot sit and think. Books think for me.' 'I called upon you this morning, and found that you were gone to visit a dying friend. I had been upon a like errand.' But the comic spirit in Lamb may come in upon his realities of feeling with instant change of note. 'There is no home for me here. There is no sense of home at Hastings. It is a place of fugitive resort, an heterogeneous assemblage of sea-mews and stock-brokers, Amphitrites of the town, and misses that coquet with the Ocean.' Such allusions as occur there, of course, make *Elia* difficult to catch in all his meaning and picturing at first glance.

'To the Shade of Elliston', written in 1831 as an *in memoriam* for an illustrious actor who had (once) played Mr. H——, might be misconsidered as a piece of artificial word-spinning, if it were not seen as an address *to* a man remarkable for his classical training and his being an actor all the time. It is a caprice, judged exactly for the occasion. It begins with an echo, and with scholarly references, to elegies of antiquity, and inwoven touches upon Elliston's merriest stage characters. Even classical hexameter and pentameter verse are heard.

Joyousest of once embodied spirits, whither at length hast thou flown? to what genial region are we permitted to conjecture that thou hast flitted?

Art thou sowing thy *Wild Oats* yet (the harvest time was still to come with thee) upon casual sands of Avernus? or art thou enacting ROVER (as we would gladlier think) by wandering Elysian streams?

In a second paper Lamb describes Elliston as he had known him, for the general reader, in a different, an explanatory rhythm and thought.

The essays in The *London Magazine* were appreciated, reprinted in other journals, toilingly imitated; and Lamb found himself invited to a banquet at the Mansion House, on the strength of them, by the Lord Mayor of London. His artistry in them might be properly perceived by the few; the many were moved by the characters whom he depicted, not least 'Bridget Elia'—but the full history of Mary Lamb would never be guessed from Elia's page.

No inescapable death-in-life molests her there, presented as Elia's cousin; she is herself a spirit of security and life for all who come.

It has been the lot of my cousin, oftener perhaps than I could have wished, to have had for her associates and mine, free-thinkers—leaders, and disciples, of novel philosophies and systems; but she neither wrangles with, nor accepts, their opinions. That which was good and venerable to her, when a child, retains its authority over her mind still. She never juggles or plays tricks with her understanding.

We are both of us inclined to be a little too positive; and I have observed the result of our disputes to be almost uniformly this—that in matters of fact, dates, and circumstances, it turns out, that I was in the right, and my cousin in the wrong. But where we have differed upon moral points; upon something proper to be done, or let alone; whatever heat of opposition, or steadiness of conviction, I set out with, I am sure always, in the long run, to be brought over to her way of thinking.

'Mackery End in Hertfordshire' (*Essays of Elia*).

VII. POSTSCRIPTS

Where the brother and sister could live was a question depending on Mary's mental health and on the provision of a nurse in emergency. In the hope of a normal home life, as well as from pure benevolence, they adopted a little girl named Emma Isola, whose grandfather taught Wordsworth Italian. She lived with them in a house they had at Islington for some years from 1823, a cottage beside Lamb's well-known stream, the New River. Their devotion to Emma was faultless, and Lamb took the greatest pains to make his knowledge of literature and his gifts as a writer serve her education and her young friendships. For Emma he compiled manuscript anthologies and wrote all sorts of verses. In the end she married Edward Moxon, one of the young men who gathered round Lamb in those years and whose life-work (Moxon became a publisher) owed some of its quality to Lamb. Perhaps Emma never saw clearly what *she* had owed to him, but once married she had small opportunity for brightening his solitariness.

Did he fall in love with her? It has been supposed. If he did, he told nobody, especially her. Charles Lamb could endure anything. Lamb came home from the East India House 'for ever', a pensioner, on 29 March 1825, and celebrated his freedom in one of his most resourceful essays, 'The Superannuated Man'. But its joy is not as peaceful as might seem; now that he had time to himself, Lamb wondered what allotment of time it would be. He did not like to think of his old office team still at it. . . . And what had time in store for Mary? At all events, while she was well, they could see something more of the country, and he could speed into town by the coach, stay with friends, read at the British Museum, call on editors.

A new house was taken at Enfield Chase in 1827, but in 1829 they became boarders next door; Mary was growing weaker, and her attacks lasted longer. It was necessary at length to return Londonwards and to board at Edmonton with Mr. and Mrs. Walden, who had previously taken care of Mary in her illnesses. Those 'encroached on her yearly': and yet there were great calms, and revivals of old bright pleasures, long walks, days with friends, new books (Mary tackled the novels. Will someone recapture her comments on Miss Austen?).

Since his retirement Lamb had not neglected to look for some sustained plan of writing, and in occasional prose and verse he produced an equivalent to what he might have done that way. His willingness to please was in part responsible for the *Album Verses* which he gave Moxon to publish in 1830. Not many poems have ever been penned in this style to surpass that called 'In My Own Album', but the volume contained a few others of a noble nature, some sonnets among them, 'Work', 'Leisure', and one more to Fanny Kelly. In 1833 Lamb wrote an allegorical lyric on the vanished world of Grecian beauty, which his young friend Keats should have been living to enjoy. His longest effort of those closing years was 'Satan in Search of a Wife', 1831, a comedy of the Devil's private life; a diversion for the writer, which should at least be read for minor brilliances of wit and versification. It is probable that Lamb's latest piece of poetry was in the gentler vein of his *Album Verses*, a pretty compliment and wish to Margaret W. on 8 October 1834.

One of Lamb's last prose pieces went into the album of Mr. Keymer, a bookseller, on 21 November 1834. 'When I heard of the death of Coleridge, it was without grief. It seemed to me that he long had been on the confines of the next world—that he had a hunger for eternity. I grieved then that I could not grieve. But since, I feel how great a part he was of me. . . .' Five weeks later, after a fall on a gravelled road, at a time when Mary was amid the darkness of one more mad period, Lamb died; he had told Mary where he would like his grave in Edmonton churchyard to be, and she managed to point out the place to his friends. Of the numerous public tributes to him which followed, none would have pleased him better (even if he had made his jokes on the circumstances) than a passage of eulogy in the annual Latin Oration at Christ's Hospital, spoken by the Senior Grecian, Joseph Christian, before the Lord Mayor and the usual parade of rank and talent in September 1835.

Mary lived on harmlessly, no longer the equal of herself in her brother's time but still able to astonish people now and then by her memory, insight, and imagination, until 1847. She lies buried in the same grave as Charles. John Lamb had died in 1821, and no reason remained why the history of Charles and Mary, so much like an Elizabethan tragedy in its principal theme, should be kept from their readers any longer. Some time after 1860, the stack of volumes in which Lamb had declared that his true Works consisted—'more MSS. in folio than ever Aquinas left, and full as useful'—the ledgers at the India House—were destroyed in a general abolition of such gear. There is grief among the research-students of to-day that this was done, and nobody has felt able to invent in Lamb's way what he may have written in verse or prose in the margins of those monumental account-books.

One group of writings by him, little noticed in this pamphlet so far, was not meant for publication any more than the India House ledgers, but has become a classic of its kind. The Letters of Lamb now in print—the edition by E. V. Lucas dated 1935 is the best—number about a thousand, and some of the long ones are singly comparable to his full-scale essays. There are readers who are more pleased with them than with the essays in general, since in their nature they are more direct and unmoderated in expression, and some of the ideas repeated in the essays come out in them with a cheerful vehemence. If it is the full story of Lamb's life and friendships that is looked for, this great series of records surpasses in its original intensity the skill of the biographer. It must miss some passages known from other sources to the modern biographer, for many letters are lost or mislaid, but that is a minor deficiency. Above all, the capability of Lamb as the friend of a multitude of people, old or young, and his equal range and fineness of mental sympathies, lie open in the Letters, and even in the short notes, which mostly have his original touch in dealing with things quite ordinary.

Lamb, the letter-writer, spoke to each recipient as to an individual, and that sympathetic gift distinguishes the very last letter he is known to have sent. It was to the homely old wife of his schoolfellow, George Dyer, and the date is five days before his death. The book in question was found, with the leaf turned down at the description of the death of Sir Philip Sidney. Mr. Cary wrote a poem to Lamb in eternity on regaining his book.

Dec. 22nd, 1834

Dear Mrs. Dyer—I am very uneasy about a *Book* which I either have lost or left at your house on Thursday. It was the book I went out to fetch from Miss Buffam's, while the tripe was frying. It is called Phillip's Theatrum Poetarum; but it is an English book. I think I left it in the parlour. It is Mr. Cary's book and I would not lose it for the world. Pray, if you find it, book it at the Swan, Snow Hill, by an Edmonton stage immediately, directed to Mr. Lamb, Church Street, Edmonton, or write to say you cannot find it. I am quite anxious about it. If it is lost, I shall never feel like tripe again.

With kindest love to Mr. Dyer and all,

Yours truly,

C. Lamb.

It was not for Lamb, notwithstanding his beginnings in literature on the poetical side and his belief through life that he was a poet and might write something next, by heaven's blessing, like a great poem, to come near his friends of the Lake School as a reformer of English poetry. But we may attribute the name that he won in prose in his own time and afterwards to a cause which can easily be overlooked. It was Lamb who more than anyone brought about an imaginative treatment of English prose in exchange for the formality and solidity of much eighteenth-century writing.

He was not a hard theorist, and he had a value for the Johnsonian and the Gibbonian traditions, but both from his disposition and his reading he rejoiced in a far larger spectrum of prose style than he first found in use. If it had been true that he had no ear for music (but his claim is soon disproved) it would still be his distinction to have heard newly the many musical possibilities of language and to have created new examples of them answering in melody or in harmony to earth's many voices.

EPILOGUE

Charles Lamb, to those who know thee justly dear
For rarest genius, and for sterling worth,
Unchanging friendship, warmth of heart sincere,
And wit that never gave an ill thought birth,
Nor ever in its sport infixed a sting;
To us, who have admired and loved thee long,
It is a proud as well as pleasant thing
To hear thy good report, now borne along
Upon the honest breath of public praise:
We know that with the elder sons of song,
In honouring whom thou hast delighted still,
Thy name shall keep its course to after days. . . .

The Times, 6 August 1830   ROBERT SOUTHEY, *Poet Laureate.*

CHARLES LAMB

A Select Bibliography

(Place of publication London, unless stated otherwise)

Bibliography:

A BIBLIOGRAPHY OF THE FIRST EDITIONS . . . OF CHARLES AND MARY LAMB, published prior to . . . 1834, by Luther S. Livingston. New York (1903).

BIBLIOGRAPHY OF THE WRITINGS OF CHARLES AND MARY LAMB, by J. C. Thomson. Hull (1908).

BIBLIOGRAPHICAL LIST (1794–1834). In *The Works.* (Vol. I), ed. T. Hutchinson (1908).

THE ASHLEY LIBRARY CATALOGUE. Vol. III, by T. J. Wise (1923).

Collected Works:

THE WORKS OF CHARLES LAMB, 2 vols. (1818).

THE POETICAL WORKS OF ROGERS, LAMB. . . . Paris (1829).

THE PROSE WORKS, 3 vols. (1835).

THE POETICAL WORKS. (1836 : 1848).

THE WORKS [ed. Sir T. N. Talfourd], 5 parts (1840), 4 vols. (1850).

ELIANA . . . HITHERTO UNCOLLECTED WRITINGS, ed. J. E. Babson. Boston (1866–7).

THE COMPLETE CORRESPONDENCE AND WORKS, ed. T. Purnell, 4 vols. (1870).

THE WORKS, ed. R. H. Shepherd (1874).

THE WORKS, ed. Charles Kent (1875).

LIFE, LETTERS AND WRITINGS, ed. P. Fitzgerald, 6 vols. (1875).

THE WORKS, ed. A. Ainger, 7 vols. (1878–8).

LIFE AND WORKS, ed. A. Ainger, 12 vols. (1899–1900).

THE WORKS, ed. W. Macdonald, 12 vols. (1903).

THE WORKS, ed. E. V. Lucas, 7 vols. (1903–5). (6 vols., 1912, including rev. edn. of Letters.)

THE WORKS, ed. T. Hutchinson, 2 vols. Oxford (1908).

COLLECTED ESSAYS, 2 vols. (1929) [Illustrated]. Gregynog Press edition.

Selected Works:

LAMB'S CRITICISM. A Selection, ed. E. M. W. Tillyard. Cambridge (1923).

EVERYBODY'S LAMB, ed. A. C. Ward (1933).

SELECTED ESSAYS, LETTERS, POEMS, ed. J. L. May (1953).

Works Written in Collaboration with Mary Lamb:

TALES FROM SHAKESPEARE, 2 vols. (1807).

MRS. LEICESTER'S SCHOOL (1807).

POETRY FOR CHILDREN (1809).

Works containing Contributions by Lamb:

FALSTAFF LETTERS (1796), ed. Sir I. Gollancz (1907) — by J. White and C. Lamb.

POEMS ON VARIOUS SUBJECTS BY S. T. COLERIDGE (1796) — contains four sonnets signed C.L.

POEMS BY S. T. COLERIDGE, Second Edition. To which are now added Poems by Charles Lamb and Charles Lloyd. Bristol (1797).

BLANK VERSE, by C. Lloyd and C. Lamb (1798).

THE POETICAL RECREATIONS OF the *Champion*, ed. J. Thelwall (1822) — contains many contributions by Lamb.

Separate Works:

A TALE OF ROSAMUND GRAY AND OLD BLIND MARGARET. Birmingham (1798).

JOHN WOODVIL, A TRAGEDY(1802).

THE ADVENTURES OF ULYSSES (1808), ed. E. A. Gardner. Cambridge (1921).

SPECIMENS OF ENGLISH DRAMATIC POETS (1808).

MR. H——, OR BEWARE A BAD NAME. Philadelphia (1813).

ELIA. Essays which have appeared under that signature in the *London Magazine* (1823).

ALBUM VERSES, WITH A FEW OTHERS (1830).

SATAN IN SEARCH OF A WIFE [anon.] (1831).

THE LAST ESSAYS OF ELIA (1833).

ELIA. Both series. 2 vols. (1835).

RECOLLECTIONS OF CHRIST'S HOSPITAL (1835).

ESSAYS OF ELIA, 2 series, ed. A. Ainger (1883); ed. L. N. Hallward and S. C. Hill, 2 vols. (1895–1900).

ESSAYS OF ELIA, ed. O. C. Williams. Oxford (1911); ed. A. H. Thompson, 2 vols. Cambridge (1913).

THE LAST ESSAYS OF ELIA, ed. E. Blunden. Oxford (1929) — contains notes by F. Page.

THE ESSAYS OF ELIA. Including ELIA and THE LAST ESSAYS OF ELIA, ed. M. Elwin (1952).

THE ESSAYS OF ELIA, ed. F. W. Robinson (1959).

Note: Lamb's early journalism, about 1800, in newspapers has not been fully documented. Later, he contributed to many periodicals, chiefly to Hunt's *Reflector* (1810–12), *Examiner* (1812–21) and *Indicator* (1819–21); the *London Magazine* (1820–5); *New Monthly Magazine* (1825–7); Hone's *Every-Day Book* (1825–6); *Table Book* (1827); *Year Book* (1831); *Blackwood's Magazine* (1828–30); *Athenæum* (1832–4).

Letters:

LETTERS, WITH A SKETCH OF HIS LIFE, ed. Sir T. N. Talfourd, 2 vols. (1837).

FINAL MEMORIALS; CONSISTING CHIEFLY OF HIS LETTERS, NOT BEFORE PUBLISHED, ed. Sir T. N. Talfourd, 2 vols. (1848).

LETTERS, ed. W. C. Hazlitt, 2 vols. (1886).

LETTERS, ed. W. Ainger, 2 vols. (1888).

LETTERS, ed. E. V. Lucas, 2 vols. (1905).

LETTERS, ed. H. H. Harper, 5 vols. Boston (1905) — the most splendid of all the editions. Many facsimiles.

THE LETTERS OF CHARLES LAMB, TO WHICH ARE ADDED THOSE OF HIS SISTER, MARY LAMB. The First Complete Edition, ed. E. V. Lucas, 3 vols. (1935). Abridged, 2 vols. (1945).

LETTERS. A Selection, ed. G. Woodcock (1950).

Note: Some letters have since come to light.

Biography and Criticism:

TABLE TALK, by W. Hazlitt, 2 vols. (1821–2).

THE SPIRIT OF THE AGE, by W. Hazlitt (1825).

LORD BYRON AND SOME OF HIS CONTEMPORARIES, by Leigh Hunt (1828). [Developed into AUTOBIOGRAPHY, 3 vols. (1850), revised 1860.]

BIOGRAPHICAL AND CRITICAL HISTORY OF THE LAST FIFTY YEARS, by A. Cunningham. Paris (1834).

CHARLES LAMB, by E. Moxon (1835).

TO THE MEMORY OF CHARLES LAMB, by W. Wordsworth. Privately printed (1835).

EARLY RECOLLECTIONS, by J. Cottle, 2 vols. (1837).

THE BOOK OF GEMS. MODERN POETS, by S. C. Hall (1838).

HOOD'S OWN (LITERARY REMINISCENCES), by T. Hood (1839).

MEMOIRS, by C. Mathew, 4 vols. (1839).

CRITICAL AND MISCELLANEOUS ESSAYS, by T. B. Macaulay, 5 vols. Philadelphia (1841–4).

AUTOBIOGRAPHY, by L. Hunt, 3 vols. (1850).

THE LIFE OF BENJAMIN ROBERT HAYDON, FROM HIS AUTOBIOGRAPHY AND JOURNALS, ed. T. Taylor, 3 vols. (1853–4).

MY FRIENDS AND ACQUAINTANCES, by P. G. Patmore, 4 vols. (1853).

LEADERS IN LITERATURE, by T. De Quincey (1862).

CHARLES LAMB. A MEMOIR, by B. W. Procter [Barry Cornwall] (1866).

CHARLES LAMB. HIS FRIENDS, HIS HAUNTS AND HIS BOOKS, by P. Fitzgerald (1866).

DIARY, by H. Crabb Robinson, 3 vols. (1869), ed. E. J. Morley, Oxford, 1927, with added material.

MARY AND CHARLES LAMB, by W. C. Hazlitt (1874).

RECOLLECTIONS OF WRITERS, by C. C. & M. C. Clarke (1878).

REMINISCENCES, by T. Carlyle, 2 vols. (1881).

CHARLES LAMB, by A. Ainger (1882).

MARY LAMB, by Mrs. Gilchrist (1883).

MISCELLANIES, by A. C. Swinburne (1886).

OBITER DICTA, by A. Birrell, Series 2 (1887).

APPRECIATIONS, by W. Pater (1889)
— contains an essay on Lamb.

IN THE FOOTPRINTS OF CHARLES LAMB, by B. E. Martin (1891).

CHRIST'S HOSPITAL. RECOLLECTIONS OF LAMB, COLERIDGE AND LEIGH
HUNT, by R. B. Johnson (1896).

THE LAMBS: THEIR LIVES, THEIR FRIENDS AND THEIR CORRESPONDENCE,
by W. C. Hazlitt (1897).

CHARLES LAMB AND THE LLOYDS, by E. V. Lucas (1898).

SIDELIGHTS ON CHARLES LAMB, by B. Dobell (1903).

WITH ELIA AND HIS FRIENDS, by J. R. Rees (1903).

CHARLES LAMB; SA VIE ET SES OEUVRES, par A. Derocquigny. Lille (1904).

CHARLES LAMB, by W. Jerrold (1905).

LECTURES AND ESSAYS, by A. Ainger, 2 vols. (1905).

LIFE OF CHARLES LAMB, by E. V. Lucas (1905).

CHARLES LAMB, by S. L. Bensusan (1910). [Illustrated].

A SURVEY OF ENGLISH LITERATURE 1780–1830, by O. Elton, 2 vols.
(1912).

CHARLES LAMB, by F. Masson (1913).
CHRIST'S HOSPITAL, A RETROSPECT, by E. Blunden (1923).

THE LETTERS OF THOMAS MANNING TO CHARLES LAMB, ed. G. A. Ander-
son (1925).

THE ELIAN MISCELLANY, by S. M. Rich (1931).

VOTIVE TABLETS, by E. Blunden (1931).

LAMB BEFORE ELIA, by F. V. Morley (1932).

CHARLES LAMB AND HIS CONTEMPORARIES, by E. Blunden. Cambridge
(1933).

CHARLES LAMB, RECORDED BY HIS CONTEMPORARIES, by E. Blunden
(1934).

THE ENGLISH FAMILIAR ESSAY IN THE EARLY NINETEENTH CENTURY, by M. H. Law. Philadelphia (1934).

THE FROLIC AND THE GENTLE, by A. C. Ward (1934).

LAMB ALWAYS ELIA, by E. C. Johnson (1935).

HENRY CRABB ROBINSON ON BOOKS AND THEIR WRITERS, by Edith Morley, 3 vols. (1938).

THE ORDEAL OF BRIDGET ELIA, by E. C. Ross (1940).

THE DISCIPLINE OF LETTERS, by G. Gordon. Oxford (1946).
'Charles Lamb and the Elizabethans', by R. C. Bald. [In *Studies in Honor of A. H. R. Fairchild*. Columbia, 1946].

THE LAMBS: A STUDY OF PRE-VICTORIAN ENGLAND, by K. S. Anthony (1948).

CHARLES LAMB AND ELIA, ed. J. E. Morpurgo (1948).

CHARLES LAMB AND HIS HERTFORDSHIRE, by R. L. Hine (1949).

CHARLES LAMB AND EMMA ISOLA, by E. C. Ross (1950).

THE ENGLISH ROMANTIC POETS AND ESSAYISTS: A REVIEW OF RESEARCH AND CRITICISM, ed. C. W. Houtchens and L. H. Houtchens. Oxford (1958).

Note: Since May, 1935 the Charles Lamb Society has issued a Monthly Bulletin. ed. S. M. Rich.